Up and Down the Worry Hill

A Children's Book about
Obsessive-Compulsive Disorder and its Treatment

By Aureen Pinto Wagner, Ph.D.   Illustrations by Paul A. Jutton

A Lighthouse Press Book

First edition April 2000
Second edition May 2004
Third edition May 2013

Library of Congress Control Number: 2004092498

Copyright© 2000-2013 by Lighthouse Press, Inc.

All rights reserved. No part of this book may be reproduced by any process whatsoever without the written permission of the copyright owner.

Published by Lighthouse Press, Inc.

www.Lighthouse-Press.com

ISBN-13: 978-0-9795392-5-1

WORRY HILL® Registered in the U.S. Patent and Trademark office.

Fourth Printing

Printed in the United States of America

A previous edition of this book
has been cataloged as follows:

Publisher's Cataloging-in-Publication

Wagner, Aureen Pinto.
   Up and down the worry hill : a children's book about obsessive-compulsive disorder and its treatment / by Aureen Pinto Wagner ; illustrations by Paul A. Jutton. -- 2nd ed
   p. cm.
   SUMMARY: Examination of compulsive behavior emphasizes that many people have this disorder and discusses its causes, effects, and treatment options.
   Audience: Ages 4-14.
   LCCN 2004092498
   ISBN-10: 0-9677347-6-2
   ISBN-13: 978-0-9677347-6-7

   1. Obsessive-compulsive disorder in children-- Juvenile literature. 2. Obsessive-compulsive disorder. I. Jutton, Paul A., ill. II. Title.

RJ506.O25W34 2004   618.92'85227
                                              QBI33-2026

CPSIA Section 103
Tracking Label for
Lead-free Compliance
Printer: Josten's Printing & Publishing
231 S. Kelsey St.
Visalia, CA 93291
Run No: 802241
Date: June 2018

To all the courageous children who have taught me about

the struggles and victories of being a child with OCD.

With thanks to my husband, Scott, who first inspired me to write this book,

and with whose continued support this book was made possible,

to our children Catherine and Ethan, and to my parents and family

for their love and confidence in me through the years.

Preface for Parents and Professionals

When children experience obsessions and compulsions, they are often scared, confused, ashamed, and defensive, as they cannot explain their uncontrollable worries and senseless rituals. **Up and Down the Worry Hill** is written to dispel the fears and uncertainties of these children. Children need to know that they are not alone and that neither they nor their parents are to blame. They need to know that help is available and that they can have a significant impact on their own treatment and recovery.

In the course of my experience in treating Obsessive-Compulsive Disorder (OCD), I developed a child-friendly approach to convey these messages to youngsters. Many parents asked me to write a book, so that other families could benefit from the same understanding of this beguiling illness. So was born **Up and Down the Worry Hill.**

Up and Down the Worry Hill describes OCD from a child's perspective. It provides accurate information about OCD and offers parents, educators and clinicians the chance to engage in an open discussion of a baffling illness. It attempts to give children with OCD a sense of control and hope. Hope and optimism are critical in building the readiness and persistence that it takes to gain mastery over OCD.

Most importantly, **Up and Down the Worry Hill** helps children prepare to engage in treatment. It describes **cognitive-behavioral therapy** (CBT), a highly effective treatment for OCD, in a manner that children can comprehend. This book uses real-life metaphors to describe the concepts of CBT. Metaphors simplify difficult and abstract concepts by comparing them to situations that children can easily understand. The metaphor of the Worry Hill evolved over the years in my work with children with OCD. Children and adults have responded very favorably to it.

The first edition of **Up and Down the Worry Hill,** published in 2000, received an overwhelming response. This third edition builds on previous editions, with more comprehensive coverage of the concepts, process and steps involved in CBT and recovery.

To make the best use of this book, read and discuss this story several times with your child. Repeated readings will help your child absorb and integrate the many complexities of OCD and CBT gradually. Young children may benefit from having segments of the book read to them at different times. Reading this book to siblings and classmates of children with OCD may help them be more empathic and supportive.

This book has two companion books that capitalize on the synergy of the parent-child-therapist team in conquering OCD. **What to do when your Child has Obsessive-Compulsive Disorder: Strategies and Solutions** offers parents and educators step-by-step practical guidance in helping children triumph over OCD. **Treatment of OCD in Children and Adolescents: Professional's Kit** provides therapists with in-depth description of the Four-Phase Worry Hill treatment approach and specific protocols for effectively treating various forms of OCD. Information on these companion books is available at the back of this book.

May your ride **Up and Down the Worry Hill** be victorious!

Aureen P. Wagner, Ph.D.

Casey woke up and rubbed his eyes. It was a bright and sunny day.

He was happy and wanted to ride the new bicycle his parents gave him. He had been practicing everyday and could ride it quite well.

Casey's dad had promised that he would teach Casey how to ride up the Big Hill at the end of the street and then coast down it. Casey had been waiting to do that for a long time. Today was the day...

Casey sat up in bed. He picked up Teddy and touched him four times.
Then he got out of bed carefully, with one foot first, then the other.

He patted his pillow four times and tucked his sheets all around it.

Casey smiled. "It feels just right. Now I'll have a perfect day."

"Mom, I'm up! I really want to ride my new bike."

"Come on down, Casey," replied his mother. "Dad and Jenny are up too.
It's time for breakfast, and then off to school you go. You can ride your bike when you
get home from school in the afternoon."

Casey started to get dressed for school. He put on his "special" pants. They felt right. Then he picked out the socks that felt good on his toes. He had many other pairs of socks but the bumps on the seams bothered his feet.

Casey was just leaving his room when he wondered if he'd said a bad word. He shook his head as he tried to shake the thought out.

He counted the stairs as he went down. "That wasn't right," he said.
He came back up and counted them again.
And again.

"I wish I could get it right the first time," Casey sighed.

Just then, a bad thought popped into his mind.

Casey shook his head and tried not to think about it. But it wouldn't go away.

9

"Look, Casey, I made muffins for you,"
said his mother, giving him a hug.
"Oh, goody! My favorite kind," grinned
Casey. "But my hands feel dirty.
I have to wash them."

Casey scrubbed his hands
well and rinsed them.
Then he looked
at them carefully.
"They still feel yucky.
What if they still have
germs on them?"
He washed his hands again.

Casey's mother came in. "Are you
done washing, dear?" Casey was getting
frustrated. "My hands feel germy.
I have to wash them again."

Casey's mother looked at his hands.
"They're very clean. Turn off the
faucet. You'll be late for school," she said.

Casey looked at his mother. "I can't! Please, can you turn it off for me?"
Casey's mother turned off the faucet and helped him out of the bathroom.

Casey sat down for breakfast after giving his dad a hug.

His sister Jenny ate her muffins fast.
His parents sipped their coffee and talked
about riding in the park on their new bicycles.

But Casey wasn't listening. He was busy cutting his muffin up into small pieces, all the same size. He ate one piece on one side of his mouth, then took one sip of milk, and ate the next piece on the other side of his mouth.

Then he repeated it all over again.

Casey's mother looked at the clock. "Hurry, Casey, it's almost time for the bus! Just take a few bites all at once and you'll be done before you know it."

Casey looked at his plate. He had seven bites left and he had to finish them in the right order.

"I can't eat any faster. I have to do it exactly this way," he whispered to himself.

Jenny laughed at him. "C'mon Casey-man, what's the matter? Can't you hurry, slow-poke?" I saw you this morning, touching and counting things in your room. You're weird, Casey!"

Casey was sad. He finished his breakfast just in time for the school bus. Then he had to check his book bag to make sure he hadn't forgotten his homework. He counted his books, pencils and erasers.

Jenny started talking just then, and Casey thought he made a mistake. He checked and counted again, just to be sure.

"Mom, you saw me do my homework, right? Did I put it in my bag?" Casey was frantic as he rushed out the door.

"Be safe, be well,
don't slip, don't fall,
goodbye, goodluck..."
Casey muttered his
goodluck charm
under his breath.

At school, the teacher, Mrs. Kelly, talked about the special project for the day.
"We're going to learn about the sun, the moon and the planets today.
Then you can draw and paint them!"

Casey was excited. He knew lots of things about the planets and he couldn't wait to say them. Then, suddenly, he felt scared. He thought about drawing and painting the planets. What if the paint got on his hands and he couldn't wash it off? Would it make him sick?

He asked Mrs. Kelly if he would get sick. "No, Casey, you'll be fine," she replied. "Are you sure, Mrs. Kelly? I won't vomit?" "You know that already, Casey. It's time to start your project." But Casey couldn't stop thinking about it.

Casey began to draw the planets. He wanted his drawing to be perfect.
The circles didn't come out right, so he erased them and drew them again.
It still wasn't perfect. Casey erased it again. The paper tore.

Casey was getting tired. The other kids had finished their drawings and
were already painting.

Everyone else was having fun. Why couldn't he be like them?
Casey felt ashamed and hid his drawing.

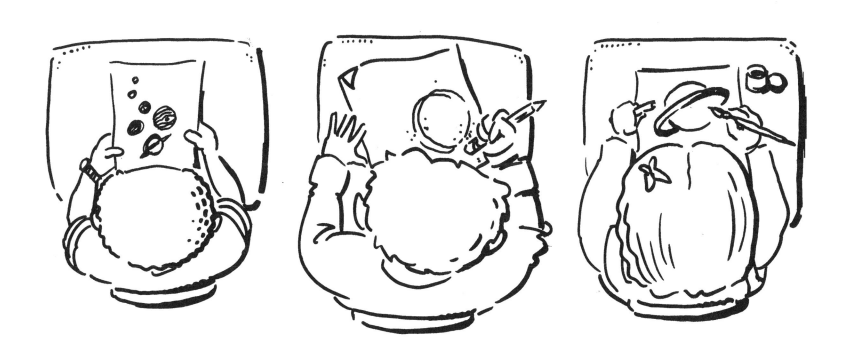

Alex and Laura were sitting next to Casey. Alex said, "Hey, how come you're always the last one to finish, Casey?" Laura leaned over and said, "Let me see your drawing! Look, the paper's torn. Why do you erase it so much?"

Casey looked away. He didn't know what to say. He wished he could hide somewhere or disappear. He couldn't wait to get home.

Mrs. Kelly came over to Casey's desk and asked if he needed help. Casey tried to hide his face. "No thanks, I'm fine," he muttered.

Finally, it was time for Casey to go home. He was exhausted. The only thing he looked forward to was riding his bicycle with his dad.

At last, Casey's dad was home from work. It was time to ride up the Big Hill! Casey and his father put on their helmets and off they went.

Dad said, "Remember, Casey, it's hard work going up a hill. You have to keep going a little at a time. I'm right here with you if you need help."

"I really want to do it, Dad! I know I can!"

As they went up the hill, Casey began huffing and puffing. He kept saying, "I can do it, little by little."

And then...

Before he knew it,
he was at the top! He
was hot and tired, but beaming.
"I did it, Daddy, I did it," he yelled out.

Then came the best part. It was time to
coast down the hill. "Now, we can enjoy the ride
down the hill," Casey's dad called out.

"Wheeee, here I come!" said Casey as he and his dad
coasted down Big Hill. The breeze blew in his face and his
hair. He was thrilled as he rode all the way down.

Casey was laughing. He hadn't had so much fun in a long time.

Casey and his father rested at the bottom of Big Hill.

"You're a great kid, Casey," smiled his father, patting him on the back.

"But Dad, the kids at school think I'm silly or crazy. I can't do anything right."

"No one gets everything right the first time, Casey.
You're not crazy, and Mom and I love you the same, no matter what."

That night, Casey's mother came to say goodnight. She sat at his bedside. "You look tired and sad, Casey. Is everything okay? I saw you checking under your bed. Mrs. Kelly said you were trying very hard to get your drawing right at school."

Casey's eyes filled with tears. "Mom, I'm scared that if I don't do things perfectly, something bad will happen. Why do I have to do that? How come Jenny doesn't need to do that? And sometimes, I think about bad things that I don't like, but I can't make the thoughts go away."

Casey's mother kissed him on the forehead. "Nobody's perfect, Casey. Each kid is different in his or her own way," she replied. "But that doesn't mean that you are not good or smart. Dad and I found a doctor we can talk to about your worries. We'll go see Dr. Greene tomorrow. She's a child psychologist and she'll know how to help us."

Casey felt better after that. He sighed with relief and went to sleep.

Casey was nervous about talking to Dr. Greene, but she was kind. She listened as Casey and his parents told her about his worries and the things he had to repeat.

"Casey, do you like doing things over again till you get them right?" asked Dr. Greene.

"No, I wish I could stop! I'd like to play and have fun like the other kids."

"What happens if you try to stop, Casey?" asked Dr. Greene.

"I feel kind of scared and weird," Casey replied. "Sometimes, I worry about bad luck, and I can't stop thinking about it. Sometimes I don't know why, but I just have to do it a certain way."

"Is there something wrong with me, Dr. Greene? Am I the only one who has to do things this way?"

"No, Casey, all of us worry and we like to do things a certain way. But, sometimes, people can't stop worrying because they have **Obsessive-Compulsive Disorder.** It's called OCD for short. Let me tell you a little bit about OCD.

You see, Casey, when you have OCD, your brain sends you a lot of worry messages that get stuck in your mind even when there's no reason to be worried.

It's like it would be if you rang the doorbell and the button got stuck. The doorbell would keep ringing and ringing and wouldn't stop. OCD is like a 'worry bell' in your brain that gets stuck and doesn't stop.

The worry thoughts that OCD sends you are called **obsessions.** You can also think of obsessions as worry tricks that your mind is playing on you.

Compulsions or **rituals** are the things you do over and over again to make the worries go away."

Casey was surprised to hear that he had OCD and that it happened in his brain. "So it's not just my fault that I do weird things, is it Dr. Greene?" he asked.

"Not at all! Having OCD is not your fault. It's not your parents' fault either. It's like having allergies or asthma—it happens to you because you're more sensitive to it. There may be other people in your family who also have OCD because they are sensitive to it.

OCD isn't something you do on purpose to get attention or because you're lazy. Sometimes, your parents, teachers and friends may think that you are just being stubborn or annoying. It's hard for them to understand that you don't want to do it, but you don't know how to stop."

Casey's parents nodded their heads. Casey smiled. Dr. Greene really did understand!

"Casey, do you know that there are many other kids and adults who have OCD? You're not the only one!

Everyone's OCD can be a little different—people can have obsessions about someone getting hurt or bad luck happening. Sometimes, they may even have thoughts that they've said or done something really bad when they actually haven't. Rituals can also be of many types, like checking things, counting, cleaning or saying sorry all the time."

Casey thought about what Dr. Greene was saying. He knew he was not alone. He knew he wasn't bad or crazy. But would he get better? Could he be like the other kids?

"Will I always have to do things over and over, Dr. Greene?"

Dr. Greene smiled. "Well, guess what? I have some good news for you! There are some ways to fix the "worry bell" in your brain when it gets stuck. One way is called **cognitive-behavioral therapy** or CBT for short.

With CBT, you will understand that you're in charge, not OCD. You can choose what you want to think and do. You will learn to face your OCD worries and do the opposite of what OCD tells you to do. You will be surprised to find that nothing bad happens! Most of all, you will find out that you are braver than you think you are!

It's a lot like riding a bicycle. Do you ride a bicycle, Casey?"

"Yes, I rode up a big hill yesterday and then I came coasting down. It was hard work to get up the hill, but lots of fun coming down," said Casey with sparkling eyes.

"Well, Casey, in the beginning, facing your fears and stopping your rituals feels like riding up a big Worry Hill because it's hard work. You huff and you puff up the hill. If you keep going and don't give up, you get to the top of the Worry Hill. Once you get to the top, you find out that your fears don't come true! Then, it's easy to ride down the hill. You can only coast down the hill if you first get to the top.

Getting to the top of the Worry Hill takes patience and hard work. The more you practice, the easier it gets.

I will teach you some exercises called **exposure** and **ritual prevention** that will help you face your fears without doing the rituals. You will learn to face your fears one step at a time. What's the best way to prepare for riding up a big hill, Casey?"

"Try some smaller hills first?" Casey ventured.

"Yes, exactly! You start with the little hills and gradually work your way up to the big ones. You get stronger with each hill, and the big hill won't seem so big anymore. In the same way, you will learn to face your fears gradually, not all at once. You will get braver and braver with each hill.

I will **guide** you, you will **ride** up and down the Worry Hill, and your parents will **rally** for you and cheer you on. We will all work together as a team to help you ride as well as you can."

"Another way to make OCD better is to take medicine. The medicine may help the worry bell in your brain work properly again. It takes a few weeks to make the OCD better, and sometimes, it takes a while to find the right medicine.

Not everyone with OCD needs medicine. Some kids need both medicine and CBT to get better. Medicine can sometimes make it easier to learn CBT, just like training wheels make it easier to learn how to ride a bicycle. But, to be in charge, you still have to learn to ride up and down the Worry Hill."

Casey sat back in his chair. Suddenly, he didn't feel crazy, scared or confused any more.

"Wow, I don't have to believe or do what OCD tells me anymore..." He liked that idea a lot. "Yes, Dr. Greene!" he exclaimed. "I want to learn the CBT exercises to make the OCD go away. I want to be in charge!"

Casey's parents were relieved. "We'll do everything to help you learn how to beat OCD," said his father.

Casey began to see Dr. Greene every week. He learned the exposure and ritual prevention exercises.

Little by little, Casey learned how to do the opposite of what OCD wanted him to do. He walked down the stairs without counting them, washed his hands only once before eating, took big bites of his muffin and went to the bus stop without checking his book bag.

Dr. Greene was right! At first, he felt worried and scared when he didn't do the rituals, but nothing bad happened! Pretty soon, the scared feeling just went away!

Casey practiced the new things he learned everyday. The more he practiced, the less worried he felt, and the easier it became. The "worry bell" didn't seem to get stuck so much anymore.

Dr. Greene also taught Casey's parents new ways to help Casey ride up and down the Worry Hill and to be patient and understanding while he learned.

"I'm in charge now, Dr. Greene," Casey burst out with pride. "You're right, Casey," replied Dr. Greene. "But remember, no matter how well you ride or how much you practice, there will be times when you wobble or fall off the bicycle. So what would you do if you fell off your bicycle?"

"I'd get up and see if I need a bandage. Or maybe I'd have to go to the doctor if I got hurt bad."

"And after you've taken care of it, would you ride your bicycle again?"

"Oh, yes, I'd get on my bicycle as soon as I could."

Dr. Greene nodded. "Casey, sometimes you may have an OCD "slip" or "fall" no matter how well you ride. It may happen when you are tired or not feeling well. It's no different than falling off a bicycle. You pick yourself up, fix the problem, and ride that Worry Hill again."

Casey started feeling a lot better. After a few weeks, he noticed that he didn't worry as much or feel sad anymore. He didn't have to touch things four times any more. He could eat his muffins just as fast as Jenny did! His clothes didn't feel so funny now. His hands didn't feel so "germy" anymore. He even forgot to check his book bag before he ran off to school!

Most of all, he found out that he didn't have to be perfect! He was having fun like the other kids.

Then one day, Casey rode his bicycle up the Big Hill all by himself! He wasn't huffing and puffing as much anymore. He got to the top quickly and looked around. He was so proud of himself. Then it was time for his favorite part—coasting down the Big Hill. As he breezed past the bushes and trees, he whistled a tune and thought to himself, "I learned how to ride up the hill and I learned how to face my OCD. I want to tell all the kids with OCD who feel alone, ashamed, and sad, 'Don't give up! You too can be brave and beat OCD by riding up and down the Worry Hill.'"

Casey sang to himself, "Up the hill, down the hill, on my new bicycle..."

ADDITIONAL RESOURCES

The Anxiety Wellness Center
Dr. Aureen Wagner's Website:
www.AnxietyWellness.com

Anxiety & Depression Association of America (ADAA)
www.adaa.org

Association for Behavioral and Cognitive Therapies (ABCT)
www.abct.org

Lighthouse Press, Inc.
www.lighthouse-press.com

International OCD Foundation
www.ocfoundation.org

Obsessive Compulsive Information Center (OCIC)
www.miminc.org

Tourette Syndrome Association
www.tsa-usa.org

Can't Attend One of Dr. Wagner's Workshops?
Now available! Live recording of one of
Dr. Wagner's most popular workshops

Worried No More:
The One-Hour Workshop for Parents
The Essential Crash Course
for Parents

Topics include:
- The Many Faces of Anxiety
- Red flags and early warning signs
- The vicious cycle of avoidance
- Parenting traps
- Scientifically-proven techniques
- The Worry Hill that helps kids conquer anxiety
- Parenting that works

Comments from Parents:

"Fantastic! Absolutely superior."

"One of the most valuable workshops ever.
I wish I learned this years ago."

For use with personal computers (PC)
with a CD-ROM drive

Audio presentation with slides

Running time approximately
1 hr., 15 minutes

Available at: Lighthouse-Press.com

What to do when your Child has Obsessive Compulsive Disorder: Strategies and Solutions

The Companion Guide to **Up and Down the Worry Hill**
For parents, adolescents and families

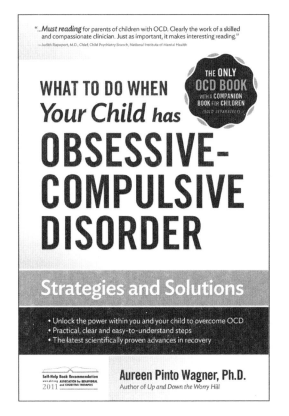

"Must reading for parents of children with OCD. Clearly the work of a skilled and compassionate clinician. Just as important, it makes interesting reading."

—Judith Rapoport, M.D., Chief, Child Psychiatry Branch, National Institute of Mental Health

Using the compelling Worry Hill approach, Dr. Wagner provides families with the blueprint to triumph over OCD.

Step-by-step practical guidance

Unlocks the power of the parent-child team to conquer OCD

Practical, clear, and easy-to-understand steps

The latest scientifically proven advances in treatment

What the experts say:

"Every parent who has a child with OCD should read this book.
I will recommend it from now on."

—Michael Jenike, M.D., Harvard Medical School

"A 'must read,' essential book…just the right balance of medical background and practical advice…filled with pearls of wisdom…"

—Roger Kurlan, M.D., Medical Advisory Board, Tourette Syndrome Association

"A truly remarkable guide for parents, clinicians and school personnel. Expertly written and organized…"

—John Piacentini, Ph.D., Director, UCLA Child OCD, Anxiety and Tic Disorders Program

Available at: Lighthouse-Press.com

Treatment of OCD in Children and Adolescents: Professional's Kit
Putting the Groundbreaking Worry Hill Treatment Approach for OCD into action!

This newly revised and expanded popular resource for professionals includes second editions of both the Therapy Manual and Teaching Tools. Dr. Wagner shares her internationally acclaimed Worry Hill protocol for OCD, along with clinical pearls from her many years of experience. She provides expert guidance on special topics including:

- Developing treatment readiness
- Collaborating with parents
- Working with reluctant children
- Overcoming treatment challenges

Benefits:

- User-friendly and appealing
- Step-by-step protocols
- Easy application and record-keeping
- Clear and self-explanatory
- Detailed case examples

"This manual is the best available resource for clinicians...clear, concise and accurate...with a rich supply of clinical insights and practical tips. I highly recommend it to all practitioners, from beginners to seasoned clinicians."

—Charles Mansueto, Ph.D., Scientific Advisory Board, Obsessive Compulsive Foundation

"This is a valuable treatment manual for youngsters with OCD. I recommend it with enthusiasm!"

—Judith Rapoport, M.D., Chief Child Psychiatry, National Institute of Mental Health

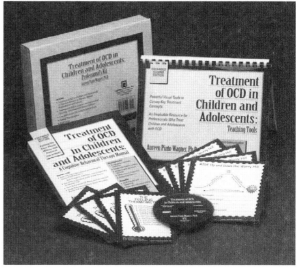

This expanded second edition includes:

1. Cognitive-Behavorial Therapy Manual
2. Complete set of thirty 8.5" x 11" Teaching Tools
3. Over 35 ready-to-print-and-use forms on CD (*PC only*)
4. Worry Hill Memory Cards and Feeling Thermometers for use in working with children and families

Worried No More: Help and Hope for Anxious Children
For parents, school personnel and healthcare professionals.

In this landmark book, Dr. Wagner provides scientifically proven and time-tested strategies to help children overcome worry, school refusal, separation anxiety, excessive shyness, panic, disasters, phobias, obsessions and compulsions.

FOR PARENTS, SCHOOL AND HEALTHCARE PROFESSIONALS

WORRIED NO MORE
Help and Hope for Anxious Children
Second Edition

- Highly Effective Practical Strategies
- Specific How-to Steps
- Clear and Easy to Understand

A masterpiece! So clear and so practical, that this is the book every school must have and every parent of a child with anxiety should read and reread...provides priceless understanding of the process of excessive anxiety and how to control it.
—John H. Greist, M.D., Distinguished Senior Scientist, Madison Institute of Medicine

Aureen Pinto Wagner, Ph.D.

Includes:

- How to tell normal anxiety from problem anxiety
- Different forms of anxiety in children and teenagers
- Red flags for anxiety
- Expressions of anxiety in school
- How to find the right professional help
- Effective treatments
- Dos and don'ts of parenting
- Step-by-step plans with examples
- Ready-to-use forms and tools
- An appealing approach to treatment

Highly acclaimed by experts:

"A masterpiece...so clear and so practical, that this is the book every school must have and every parent of a child with anxiety should read and reread...provides priceless understanding of the process of excessive anxiety and how to control it."

—John H. Greist, M.D., Distinguished Senior Scientist, Madison Institute of Medicine

"A very helpful and practical book... immensely helpful...I highly recommend it!"

—Michael Jenike, M.D., Harvard Medical School

"This excellent book could not be timelier considering the recent highly stressful events in our country. Scientific, yet highly readable, for professionals and non-professionals."

—Sara S. Sparrow, Ph.D., Professor and Chief Psychologist, Yale University Child Study Center

Available at: Lighthouse-Press.com

Worried No More:
Teaching Tools and Forms on CD

This companion toolkit helps school professionals and therapists put **Worried No More** into action with children and families. It provides a focal point for building treatment readiness and conveying key treatment concepts. It can also be used often for review during treatment.

Benefits:

- Powerful visual teaching tools
- Appealing to children and families
- Convenient, easy to use
- Enhances record-keeping
- Increases motivation and compliance
- Improves communication and learning

Sample Forms

- The Feeling Thermometer
- Parent-Teacher Log
- Home Behavior Observations
- School Behavior Observations
- My Thoughts and Feelings
- My Fear Ladder
- Exposure Progress Record
- The Worry Hill Memory Card
- Facing My Fears

Sample Teaching Tools

- About Anxiety
- The Feeling Thermometer
- How Anxiety Gets Worse
- How Thoughts Affect Feelings
- How Anxiety Can Make You Think
- The Brain and Anxiety
- How Anxiety Can Make You Act
- The Vicious Cycle of Escape
- What Parents May Naturally Do
- 3 Things to Bring Down Your Feeling Temperature
- Up and Down the Worry Hill
- Parenting Strategies
- Appropriate Attention
- Calming Space and Calming Actions
- Calm Thinking and Bravery
- Handling Meltdowns

This expanded third edition includes:

—33 Teaching Tools (8.5"x 11" color flip cards)

—Ready-to-use Microsoft® PowerPoint® slides

—Ready-to-print-and-use Forms on CD

—Feeling Thermometers

Software for use with PCs only

Available at: Lighthouse-Press.com

Anxiety and OCD at School:
Live Workshop for School Professionals

PC CD-ROM Version

Anxiety and OCD at School

2nd Edition

Workshop
For
School
Professionals

"On a scale of 1 to 10, this was a definite 10!"

"Great, great speaker! Best workshop I have attended in 28 years as a professional."

Aureen Pinto Wagner, Ph.D.

For use with personal computers (PC)
with a CD-ROM drive
Printable handout

This workshop is ideal for a broad range of school staff, including:

- School Psychologists
- Counselors
- Social Workers
- Speech and Occupational Therapists
- Nurses
- Mainstream and Special Education Teachers

An audio and slide presentation recorded during one of Dr. Wagner's most popular workshops for school professionals. Just like a real workshop, you'll listen to Dr. Wagner as you view the slides that accompany the presentation, and follow along with the handout. Packed with practical advice, you'll want to listen to this presentation repeatedly. This CD is ideal for staff development trainings or inservices. Dr. Wagner is a highly engaging and sought-after speaker whose workshops consistently receive outstanding reviews. You'll benefit from her many years of working with anxious children, her user-friendly conceptualizations and her practical *Worry Hill* innovations.

Comments from Participants

"On a scale of 1 to 10, this was a definite 10! Most helpful were the practical strategies for anxiety."

"Great, great speaker! Best workshop I have attended in many years (in 28 years as a professional)."

Available at: Lighthouse-Press.com

Anxiety and OCD Workshops

Dr. Aureen Wagner offers a variety of workshops on anxiety and OCD for Parents, Schools, and Healthcare Professionals.

Testimonials from participants:

"Thank you for the wonderful workshop you presented on anxiety. . . I was extremely pleased with the turnout and the response. Thank you for all your time and effort in tailoring your presentation to meet our needs."

"This was an excellent workshop on OCD. Information was presented in a thorough, concrete manner to 'grip' the attention of a diversely trained audience. I fully appreciated the inclusion of the discussion on adolescents, especially high school age students."

"This is easily one of the best workshops I have ever attended. Thank you for the wonderful touch and the tremendous knowledge you bring to us. "Excellent presentation! Very helpful – warm, articulate and positive. Nice balance of lecture—large/small group."

Visit AnxietyWellness.com for a complete description of workshops

Expert Clinician Consultation

Dr. Aureen Wagner provides consultation and supervision for healthcare professionals on assessment and treatment of anxiety disorders in children and adolescents. Consultation is tailored to suit your individual or group's needs.

Topics:

- Assessment
- Differential diagnosis
- Treatment plans
- Exposure hierarchies
- Cognitive strategies
- Socratic technique
- Treatment reluctance
- Challenges in treatment

For more information on fees and scheduling, please visit AnxietyWellness.com

Telephone Sessions are scheduled via mutual convenience.

Special Offers

The Worry Hill Master Set For the Treatment of OCD
by Aureen Pinto Wagner, Ph.D.

Includes:

- Up and Down the Worry Hill
- What to do when your Child has OCD
- Treatment of OCD in Children and Adolescents: Professional's Kit

  —Cognitive-Behavioral Therapy Manual
  —Complete set of thirty Teaching Tools (8.5"x11")
  —Over 35 ready-to-print-and-use Forms on CD (PC only)
  —Worry Hill Memory Cards and Feeling Thermometers

The Anxiety Treatment Master Set For the Treatment of Anxiety Problems
by Aureen Pinto Wagner, Ph.D.

Includes:

- Worried No More
- Worried No More: Teaching Tools and Forms on CD

  —33 Teaching Tools (8.5"x11" color flip cards)
  —Ready to use Microsoft® PowerPoint® slides
  —Ready-to-print-and-use Forms on CD (PC only)
  —Feeling Thermometers

Available at: Lighthouse-Press.com

Special Offers

The School Professionals Master Set
by Aureen Pinto Wagner, Ph.D.

Includes:

- Up and Down the Worry Hill
- Worried No More
- Worried No More:
  Teaching Tools and Forms on CD
- Anxiety and OCD at School:
  Live Workshop for School Professionals. PC CD-ROM

SAVE!
Special set pricing
at
Lighthouse-Press.com

Feeling Thermometers
Various colors and sizes

Worry Hill Memory Cards

Available at: Lighthouse-Press.com

Free!

A printed color card of the
Feeling Thermometer
for easy use with your child

While supplies last

To customers in the USA only

To receive one, please send an email to
CustomerService@Lighthouse-Press.com with:

"Send Feeling Thermometer"
in the subject line of the message.

Please indicate the name of the book
in which you saw this offer
and provide your name and mailing address
in the body of the message

DR. AUREEN PINTO WAGNER is Director of The Anxiety Wellness Center in Cary, NC, and is an Adjunct Associate Professor in the Department of Psychiatry at the University of North Carolina at Chapel Hill School of Medicine. She is also a member of the Scientific Advisory Board of the International OCD Foundation and its Pediatric Subcommittee. Dr. Wagner is a clinical child psychologist whose unique Worry Hill® approach to making cognitive-behavioral therapy accessible to youngsters has gained her international recognition. She is the author of several highly acclaimed books. **Up and Down the Worry Hill,** her first book, was written for children with OCD and their families. It was followed by **What to do When Your Child has Obsessive-Compulsive Disorder: Strategies and Solutions,** for parents and schools, and **Treatment of OCD in Children and Adolescents: Professional's Kit,** for therapists. These three books comprise the only integrated set of resources for children with OCD, their parents and their therapists.

Dr. Wagner's fourth book, **Worried No More: Help and Hope for Anxious Children** provides parents and professionals with highly effective strategies to help children who experience separation anxiety, school refusal, excessive shyness, worries, phobias and panic. **Worried No More: Teaching Tools and Forms on CD** helps professionals put it into action.

Dr. Wagner received her education at St. Agnes College, the University of Iowa, Yale University Child Study Center, and Brown University. She is a highly engaging and sought-after speaker whose workshops for clinicians, school professionals and parents consistently receive outstanding reviews.

PAUL JUTTON is an artist and illustrator living in Washington, D.C. He studied graphic design at the Rochester Institute of Technology.